Behaviour In Pre-school Groups

Contents

Introduction		2
Chapter 1	**The pre-school environment**	3
Chapter 2	**Behaviour and development**	12
Chapter 3	**Defining problems**	17
Chapter 4	**Assisting change**	26

by Ann Henderson

Acknowledgements to Hannah Mortimer

Produced by CPL Associates, London.

Introduction

When we tell children to 'Behave!' we are not giving a very clear instruction. Children's 'behaviour' includes everything they do: their approach to work and play; the ways they relate to other people; their responses to all the experiences they encounter in the world.

Young children have to learn about appropriate behaviour just as they learn other things, and the adults who care for them usually know what kinds of behaviour they want their children to learn. As parents and pre-school leaders, we want children to:

- have the motivation which will enable them to reach their full potential in all areas of development
- treat themselves and other people with respect
- be able to gain and give friendship and affection
- find acceptable ways of expressing their feelings
- make a useful contribution to the groups in which they live – the family, the pre-school and the wider community.

For most children, pre-school is the first step into the world beyond the home. This unfamiliar situation offers new challenges to children's behavioural skills, but it also provides support. The safe and stable environment of a pre-school, with plenty of adults to guide and monitor behaviour, can give children a framework within which they can construct for themselves patterns of behaviour which will serve them well in the years to come, both in school and beyond.

Chapter 1
The pre-school environment

There is not much giving of orders in a good pre-school, but there is certainly order. An ordered environment creates situations in which:

- children know what is expected of them
- each individual enjoys maximum freedom without threatening the freedom or enjoyment of others
- a familiar structure sustains a calm and purposeful atmosphere
- observant adults ensure that each child's needs are met
- mutual courtesy and kindness make it easy for people to play and work together
- children can develop self-discipline.

Positive support

Parents and pre-school workers will usually agree about the behaviour they want to encourage among the children. This will probably include:

- respecting themselves and one another
- helping taking care of the group's property
- accepting the authority of the adults in charge
- observing the rules of the group, especially any related to safety
- being willing to share and take turns
- showing kindness to younger, smaller or less able children
- engaging fully in play and learning activities.

As with any other aspect of the pre-school curriculum, the adults will need to agree about the strategies they will use to support and encourage this desirable behaviour.

The most effective strategy for ensuring that a particular piece of behaviour is repeated is to reward it. The "reward" that most children seek and which is most successful in reinforcing their behaviour is adult attention. Children need our attention in order to thrive. They prefer positive attention – smiles, hugs, verbal approval – but even negative attention is better than nothing and can still reinforce behaviour which triggers it.

This has important implications for the behaviour of the adults in the group. There is a tendency for parents and pre-school workers to leave children to their own devices when they are being "good" and to focus a lot of attention on them the minute they break the rules. This is understandable, but it does tend to leave desirable behaviour unrewarded and to give children the attention they want and need in return for behaving in undesirable ways.

It can take a deliberate shift in the adult approach in order to ensure that children receive attention when they concentrate on a task, when they are polite and helpful in the group or when they co-operate well in taking turns with other children. It is all too easy, especially with a child whose behaviour causes anxiety or disruption, to give her intensive one to one adult attention whenever she does something undesirable and to abandon her with a sigh of relief as soon as she starts being "good." Such a child quickly learns that the way to meet her need for adult attention is to be as disruptive as possible.

The skills children need

In a supportive environment in which their individual qualities and achievements are fully recognised, children can be helped to go on to the next stage when they are ready. This is as true of behaviour as it is in other areas of learning and development. Ordinary pre-school activities offer opportunities for children to practise:

Chapter 1. The pre-school environment

- ## Taking turns

    Children progress at different rates from the infant stage of needing instant gratification to the more mature child's ability to postpone for a while what he or she wants to do.

    The task of waiting can be made possible by gearing it to each child's readiness. A very young or immature child may need one-to-one adult company while waiting for her turn on the slide. Younger children need very brief turn-taking games – board games with just two players, for example, or musical instruments passed around a very small group – until they gradually become able to wait for longer periods.

- ## Sharing

    A child accustomed to ownership of all the toys at home can find it hard to understand, on first joining a pre-school group, that the equipment is to be shared and may not always be available for her sole use. Equipment which needs more than one child to make it work – two-person vehicles, for example – and games such as dominoes or picture lotto, which are more fun with someone else, will help introduce children to the advantages as well as the disadvantages of sharing.

    A well equipped pre-school, offering plenty of choice, makes sharing easier and adults will ensure that no one group or individual dominates one piece of equipment to the exclusion of other children.

- ## Politeness

    Words such as "please", "thank you" and "excuse me" will be part of some children's vocabulary before they arrive in pre-school. Other children will need the guidance and good example of adults in order to learn how to use phrases of this sort as an outward expression of politeness and concern for other people.

    Similarly, children will arrive in pre-school with a range of habits and expectations with regard to sharing food. The group will want to encourage children, for example, to pass the pieces of apple around and not to take more than their share, while bearing in mind that the skills and practices connected with eating vary from family to family and from culture to culture. The practices taught in the group must not bring children into conflict with their own families, or lead them to think that the behaviour taught at home, with regard to mealtime or other occasions, is in any way "wrong." Snacks and meals shared by a small group of children and a familiar adult, perhaps a keyworker, make it possible for the sharing of food to be a pleasant occasion as well as an opportunity to develop social skills.

Pre-school leaders working with children from cultures other than their own need to be aware that what is considered polite among one group of people may have the opposite effect on others. The eye contact which is required in conversation in Western culture, for example, is considered improper in some Eastern ones.

• Making choices

In pre-school, children have lots of opportunities to choose – between activities and, frequently, within activities. They decide whether to go on to the climbing frame or sit in the book corner and then, if they choose the book corner, they select the book. In a good pre-school they will often be encouraged to discuss with one of the adults the reasons for that choice and what they intend to do. These opportunities to choose and express intention are very important to children. They allow children to feel in control, which is a necessary experience as children move from the dependency of infancy to taking an increasing amount of responsibility for themselves. As adults give children guidance in accepting the consequences of choice, children also develop an increasing sense of responsibility towards the group and their own actions within it. Becoming aware of the importance of cause and effect in human behaviour can help children to recognise the ways in which their own behaviour will influence the actions and attitudes of those around them. This in turn will help them to make responsible choices about the conduct of their own lives.

Chapter 1. The pre-school environment

- ## The pattern of the day

    Although pre-schools need a flexible approach to the timetable, in order to be able to seize upon unexpected opportunities for pleasure or learning, they also need to create a stable and familiar environment in which children feel secure. Knowing what happens when within their group helps give children a feeling of ownership of the group. It is easier within this secure framework for children to recognise what is expected of them and also to help them develop a feeling of commitment to the wellbeing of the group and to be aware of their own part in this.

- ## Handling conflict

    There are techniques for handling conflict that can be learnt. Children often need help initially to recognise the source of conflict, even though this may be obvious to the adult. If, for example, Sita wants the blocks to build with and John wants to use them as "groceries" in the shop, there may be a quarrel. Children do not always find it easy to see situations from someone else's viewpoint, especially when they are angry and upset, and each child may be full of indignation at having her or his own purposes thwarted. They might need adult help to recognise that there is nothing wrong with what either of them wants to do, and that the problem arises from the fact that they want to use the same equipment at the same time for different purposes. An adult who can simply spell this out for them, without making any value judgements about the situation, will be teaching them a technique for approaching any similar situations in the future.

    Once they have been helped to see the nature of their problem children will often be willing to be involved in seeking solutions for it. If they cannot by themselves see any way out of the problem, the adult may perhaps suggest alternatives. The adult in this particular situation may suggest looking in the cupboard for additional blocks so that each child can pursue his or her own project without coming into conflict with the other. Another possibility might be that the children join together, first of all to build with the blocks and, secondly, to play shops together. If the adult also suggests as a possibility that the blocks be simply put away for now, this also might help to clear the children's minds about what it is they most want. A solution which the children have reached together will be much easier for them to accept and work with than one imposed from outside by the adult. The process will also provide a useful message for them about the fact that conflict can be resolved without quarrels if they tackle it together.

The rules of the group

In order to ensure that the children can cope with the rules of the group, it is important that there should not be too many rules. The adults in the staff team or the management committee need to be clear about what is most important and to limit the rules to essentials. If many of the rules seem to be designed simply to keep children safe, it may be that the group needs to look afresh at its equipment and layout in order to create a safe environment that does not rest upon too many regulations.

Once the rules are established, they need to be known.

It is helpful for both children and parents who are new to the group if the rules – and the thinking behind them – are known in advance. Some groups ensure that the rules are written as part as the introductory leaflet prepared for newcomers and discussed between parents and key worker before the child joins the group. It is then possible for the child's parents to talk through with the child before attending the group the kinds of behaviour which will be required there. This makes it easier for both parent and child. It also gives an opportunity for discussion in advance if there appears to be any conflict between the rules of the group and the behaviour which is expected or encouraged at home. The group's general policies on behaviour and discipline should be agreed at a general meeting and reviewed annually. This ensures that all parents have the opportunity to make an input.

Parents familiar with the rules can help their child to settle in the group by talking the child through what is required during the initial settling period until the rules are familiar. This protects the child from the unhappy situation of finding that he/she has done something wrong

Chapter 1. The pre-school environment

unintentionally because nobody explained in advance what was required.

Not only parents, but all the adults involved in the group in any way – including those who come in on a short term basis – need to know what the rules are and what their part must be in enforcing them. The rules may well vary from one group to another and this does not matter at all and will reflect different circumstances, layout and priorities, but it is absolutely essential that the rules do not vary within the group from day to day or from person to person. To have rules inconsistently applied creates confusion and unhappiness.

This makes meetings amongst the adults, especially the staff team, very important. All the adults involved must be confident about the rules and the thinking behind them, and should express them in an agreed way. The children must be confident that if some piece of behaviour is not acceptable, then it is never acceptable, no matter what day of the week it is or which adults are in charge. Unless this is the case, children will find it very hard really to believe in the rules and may well experiment in order to establish where the limits of acceptable behaviour really are. The adults must take great care to give clear messages to the children. If a particular kind of behaviour is unacceptable, for example, the adults need to show it – not just in words, but in body language and tone of voice. Mixed messages will confuse the children and may prolong the unwanted behaviour.

"Do as I do"

The adults have a crucial role to play not only in enforcing rules but also in providing a model of the kind of behaviour they want to encourage among the children.

Adults have great power over children and the adults' behaviour within the group is a constant demonstration of the uses to which power can be put and the ways in which it should be used. If the powerful adults in the group show courtesy and respect both for the children and for one another, this has a positive influence on the atmosphere in the group.

By the ways they handle the group's equipment, the adults demonstrate how they value it. If they show that they care for it, because it is important to the children and also because the group had to pay for it, the children will "catch" the same attitudes of care and respect for property. This will be further encouraged in a group where everyone picks up equipment which is dropped, returns books to the right place after use and leaves the jigsaws complete and ready for someone else.

In addition, adults demonstrate by their behaviour towards one another how people within this group are meant to interact. If they support and help one another, show pleasure in one another's company and reinforce one another's value and authority, they create a model of behaviour which children can profitably copy in their dealings with one another.

Within an environment in which care and courtesy are the norm, children can be supported in developing the skills and attitudes which will help them behave in ways which are acceptable to other people and satisfying to themselves.

Self-discipline

We want children to accept adult authority in the group, but we also – and perhaps more importantly – want them to develop the control, sense of direction and responsibility for their actions which will enable them to conduct their own lives in ways which are of benefit to them and to the society in which they live.

In pre-school, children are supported in making choices, and in living with the consequences of those choices. They are encouraged to talk through what they plan to do and how their plans have worked out. They are invited to select an appropriate activity and then have adult help in meeting the challenges imposed by that activity until it is completed to the child's satisfaction. The adult will be available to discuss the progress of the activity and to support the child in reviewing the approach or in celebrating an achievement.

Chapter 1. The pre-school environment

Children with a limited concentration span will be encouraged by adult company, support and conversation gradually to extend the amount of time they can give to one activity, and to appreciate the extra pleasure and satisfaction which can come from this.

Very often, children are involved also in making choices about the life of the group itself: about proposed outings, for example, or what to cook, or the selection of library books.

In all of these ways, children are supported in taking charge of their own lives and in feeling that they have a part to play in the life of the group. This leads to the kinds of self-motivated activity which form the basis for self-discipline.

Chapter 2
Behaviour and development

We all know without thinking about it that children's limited physical size, strength and skill prevent them from attempting many adult tasks. It is easier to forget that children's immaturity and inexperience also limit them in other ways, especially with regard to social behaviour.

Concepts

Intellectual immaturity can make some forms of 'good' behaviour difficult for children:

- Children who do not yet have a sufficiently clear grasp of number and volume to be able to estimate quantities find it very difficult to take their 'fair' share of a large amount of clay or Lego. "Fairness" involves mentally assessing the volume/quantity available and then dividing that by the number of children present, a mathematical exercise quite beyond most young children.

- Children too young to understand the concept of time, to recognise the vocabulary of time or to estimate the speed at which time passes will find it genuinely hard to take turns. When they want, for example, to use the tricycle, the only thing they know for sure is that they don't have it at the moment. A stopwatch, kitchen timer or sand timer which makes the passage of time visible can make waiting possible by putting it in a framework the child can understand.

- Coping with the absence of a parent/carer is also very difficult for a child who cannot conceive of the passage of hours, perhaps of a whole day. A very young or immature child may not even

Chapter 2. Behaviour and development

understand that a person who is no longer present can still continue to exist and will reappear later. A child in this position will need a lot of understanding support in order to be 'good' while awaiting the return of a parent.

Language

The rules which govern acceptable behaviour in a new situation have to be passed on to each child by means of language. If the rules are written down, they are inaccessible in that form to small children and have to be explained by the adult. Even then, the accent and vocabulary – even the language – may be so different from the familiar speech of home as to make little impact on a child.

Styles of speech also vary. A child accustomed to hearing a single clear 'no' when she behaves inappropriately may not realise at first that a complicated sentence beginning, 'We don't do that in here because...' is in fact a command. Even a command worded in a familiar way may not be recognised when spoken in a different tone of voice. Similarly, a child whose comprehension is limited to simple sentences will find it very difficult to disentangle a complex series of instructions such as 'When you've finished that, John, put it over there and then hang up your apron and go and sit on the mat.'

Some children may in addition have undetected hearing problems – or temporary hearing loss due to infection – and may appear uncooperative when they have simply not heard requests or instructions.

Concentration

Very young children cannot concentrate for very long periods of time. Paying attention throughout a 20 minute story is simply *not* possible for a child with an attention span of 6 minutes. The activities and adult support provided in pre-school can help children gradually expand the span of their attention, but obliging them to remain passive throughout a session which is much too long for them introduces the danger of teaching them not to concentrate.

Toiletting

Children acquire bladder and bowel control at varying ages, as their sphincter muscles and central nervous systems mature. Until that time 'accidents' are inevitable, especially when children are particularly absorbed in play or trying to cope with a new situation.

Toiletting accidents can also be caused by practical problems with clothing. Young children's hands are not always skilful at handling stiff buttons or unfamiliar zips, especially when in a hurry, and this often causes problems for children who are wearing new clothes – perhaps because going to pre-school is an important event.

Some children find the unfamiliar toilets in large halls rather frightening at first and may need adult company – and explanation, if the flushing system is different from the one at home.

Exploration

Children instinctively want to learn – initially by means of exploration. They need to use their senses to come to terms with all aspects of their physical environment. This makes some aspects of 'good' behaviour difficult for them when they are very young. They cannot learn about the world in theory, only from personal experience, and have to touch things with their mouths and fingers in order to understand them. This gets children into trouble – and sometimes into danger – in shops and homes. The rich resources of a good pre-school, where children find an abundance of materials which can safely be explored, can support good behaviour:

- by providing a safe outlet for children's instinctive explorations
- by giving them confidence that they can be 'good' and that their attempts to meet their own basic needs are not necessarily a source of trouble.

Chapter 2. Behaviour and development

In dealing with people, also, children experiment and explore in order to find out where the boundaries lie between acceptable and unacceptable behaviour. In an unfamiliar situation, or if the boundaries are not clear to them, children will experiment with different kinds of behaviour until it is clear to them where the lines are drawn. In an environment in which the rules are clearly explained and consistently enforced, this sort of situation should not arise, or should be resolved very quickly. Once children know clearly what they are allowed to do and what is not permitted, and have discovered that the same rules apply all the time, they have then established the situation to their own satisfaction and can direct their energies elsewhere.

In addition, some children try to test themselves, discovering through experiment the development of their own physical skills and courage. Dangerous games such as 'How many steps can I jump down?' often arise from this desire to explore. Children need safe outlets for physical energy and acceptable challenges to their ever-expanding range of skills. In pre-school, with a keyworker alert to each child's development, each new accomplishment will be celebrated and appropriate new challenges set.

New people, new places

Young children's experience is necessarily very limited and, like adults, children can be thrown off the course of their usual behaviour by the need to adjust to the unfamiliar:

- The acoustics in a large room full of hard surfaces – perhaps the first public building the child has been in – are very different from those in a small home containing carpets or upholstery. Children's hearing is very sensitive and the unexpectedly harsh noises can terrify some of them. Others react with noisy over-excitement, irritability or weepiness. The addition of rugs and cushions in at least some areas of the pre-school can be very helpful in toning down the noise level and helping children to cope with it without becoming noisy themselves.
- The presence of a number of unfamiliar people is initially stressful for many children. Children, like adults, react to stress in different

ways: some become timid; others may for a while 'show off'. The use of the key worker system, which ensures that each child can quickly become familiar with one special adult in the group, can help children over these initial 'teething troubles'.

- Children who are accustomed only to 'rough and tumble' play with children at home may need adult company at first to show them that there are other ways of enjoying companions.
- The presence of 'wide open spaces' indoors, for children accustomed to small rooms, can make some children timid and trigger over-excited behaviour in others. A layout which divides up the space into defined activity areas can help all children, and encourage more settled play.

New rules

During their first years at home, children often build up quite a clear picture of what kinds of behaviour are expected and permitted there. When they come into pre-school, however, the rules may change. In particular, some activities which may for good reason not be permitted at home may be allowed or even encouraged in pre-school. Play with water, for example, or messy materials such as clay or finger paint, is an important part of the pre-school curriculum but may not be possible at home. It can be very hard for a child who finds that some of the familiar rules have apparently disappeared to understand that other rules – about not hurting other people, for example - still apply. Children new in the group often need one to one support for a while – perhaps from their keyworker – to talk them through the organisation of this unfamiliar place until they understand clearly what is allowed and what is not.

Adult awareness of the general process of child development, combined with close observation of individual children, will ensure that in this, as in other areas of activity, the targets we set for our children are reasonable ones, and that children have the support they need in moving on to fresh challenges when they are ready.

Chapter 3
Defining problems

It is all too easy to categorise other people and their behaviour as a "problem". Adults in pre-school need to be really clear about the behaviour they expect of both adults and children and about the distinction between behaviour which poses a problem for the adults and behaviour which, much more seriously, might be an indication of a problem for the child.

Problems for adults

For some adults in some circumstances, children can present a "problem" simply by being healthy, active, enquiring children. If children are exuberant, active, full of fun, seeking new challenge and excitement everywhere, this should not be a problem in a pre-school group. If energy, initiative and good health present problems, then there is something wrong with what is being provided for the children. More demanding challenges, both physical and intellectual, may be needed for a child or a group of children who seem to be wanting to generate extra excitement for themselves.

Noise can sometimes appear to be a problem in a large group. Certainly, excessive noise can disturb other people's concentration and may be unpleasant or alarming for younger children. However, exploring with their voices and the sounds their own bodies can produce is a legitimate area of activity for children. It should be possible to reduce overall noise and create some quiet areas in pre-school by making every effort to introduce sound absorbing materials such as rugs, cushions and, if possible, curtains.

Some adults who are not very confident of their own authority feel challenged and uneasy when faced with children who are reluctant always to conform to adult requests and requirements. There is a balance to be achieved here. The adults are responsible for the overall conduct of the group and must ensure that the behaviour of some children cannot spoil the pleasure and learning of others. At the same time, it is important to remember that total and indiscriminate obedience is not always in itself a good thing. We want our children to grow up with the judgement and independence to consider the requests and commands they receive and, sometimes, to say no. There will be times in their lives when they ought to feel able to resist invitations from their peers, and sometimes to protect themselves from inappropriate approaches by adults, by having the confidence to refuse.

In order to achieve the children's co-operation whilst still allowing them to retain and develop a sense of independence and autonomy, pre-school workers will be careful to explain to children not just what the rules are, but the thinking behind them. Sometimes, it may be appropriate to discuss the rules with all the children together as a group and to invite their comments. This enables the adults to pick up any misunderstandings that the children may have about the way the group is run and can also help the children to see the group as theirs. It is much easier for them to accept and understand the rules if they feel that they have had a part in the thinking behind them and even in helping to make them. Even very young children can be surprisingly mature and thoughtful when they are invited to take part in this way in the administration of their own group – and can indeed be very effective in ensuring that their friends keep to the rules once they have all approved and understood them.

Problems for children

Some kinds of behaviour, whether or not they are challenging for the adults in the group, may be an indication of problems for the child. Behaviour of this kind demands close and serious attention.

In order to make reliable judgements about behaviour – as about anything else – plenty of clear, accurate information is needed. When children behave in an inappropriate or worrying way, the adults involved may well become upset or angry and this is not the frame of

Chapter 3. Defining problems

mind in which to make judgements. If any child's behaviour gives frequent or consistent cause for concern, a system of objective observation needs to be established in order to gather as much and as accurate information about the child as possible. Detailed observation systems are described in the Pre-school Learning Alliance publication, *"Observation and Record Keeping – A Curriculum for Each Child."* Many pre-schools use regular observation systems to monitor each child's development and progress. For groups which have not yet begun to do this, it is easy to instigate observations of a specific child. If a particular type of behaviour gives cause for concern, the most useful immediate observation system is to record each time that piece of behaviour occurs, together with what happened immediately beforehand and what happened immediately afterwards. If this information is gathered over a period of time, recording exactly what happens, without judgements or interpretations, it can throw up illuminating insights into the causes of the behaviour. It may become apparent, for example, that this child always behaves in this way in response to a particular situation. It may be, on the other hand, that the behaviour in question always gives rise to a particular outcome. Perhaps the behaviour always results in a sudden input of adult attention.

An objective record of this kind can be very helpful in focusing the adults' minds on the true nature of the problem. If, after observation, it becomes clear that the problem is one the group cannot cope with alone, the observation records that have been built up will be of enormous value to any outside professional the group needs to call in.

There are several kinds of behaviour which might give pre-school staff and parents cause for concern:

• Age-inappropriate behaviour

Aspects of behaviour which are developmentally appropriate at some stages of children's lives may give rise to concern at other times.

Tantrums, for example, are very common among toddlers. The child has not yet acquired a sufficient grasp of language to be able to express feelings in words. At the same time, the child's feelings can be very powerful – even overpowering. The urge to explore and the need to begin to assert independence often bring the child into conflict with powerful adults and the resulting frustration, having no other outlet, spills over into a tantrum. The sudden, overwhelming feelings of anger and frustration can be alarming to the child as well as to the adult and a very young child may need comfort combined with restraint. Pre-schools and parents can help by providing outlets for violent emotions – natural materials such as clay to bang, and various kinds of music to listen and respond to. In addition, books and stories can help the child to see that other people experience the same feelings, that the feelings have a name and can be talked about. Gradually, the child finds other ways of expressing frustration. A child who continues to have tantrums long after other children of the same age have stopped, or who goes back to having them after an interval, deserves some special attention. Some children begin to use tantrums as a means of manipulating the adults around them and they too may need support in obtaining the attention they want in more acceptable ways.

Biting also is common among very young children. Small children naturally use their mouths as a means of exploration and a young or very small child with no other weapons might begin to find that biting is a useful way of defending herself or making her presence felt amongst a number of older or larger children.

Later, a child may revert to immature biting behaviour under pressure of anger, excitement or, even, a sudden upsurge of affection. Biting is painful and must be stopped or prevented, but these occasional lapses need not in themselves give rise to great concern, though the adults may wish to observe the child to check for other signs of immaturity or regression.

In general, adults will be concerned about a child whose behaviour is that of a much younger child. On rare occasions, behaviour characteristic of older people will also give rise to concern. A very young child initiating sexual games, or activities which show precocious sexual understanding, may sometimes be giving an indication of sexual abuse and must be observed carefully, the observations being kept in a confidential file.

It must always be remembered that children develop at different rates. A child with disabilities or learning difficulties may show behaviour characteristic of much younger children and will need the support and encouragement which belong with that stage of development, regardless of the child's chronological age.

• Disruption

Children who are busily engrossed in play will sometimes accidentally disrupt the activities of other children because they are too busy thinking about their own concerns. This should be discussed with the children concerned and may have implications for the layout of the room.

Disruption or damage to other children's activities caused repeatedly and deliberately is a different matter. Some children, whose attention span or understanding of the activities is very limited, may feel generally unable to do anything with the equipment beyond knocking down the constructions, splashing with the water or tossing about the collage materials. This child needs one-to-one adult support in order to find a "way in" to the activities which will be more satisfying for the child as well as less disruptive for other people. There may also be a need to help this child to build up relationships with other children so that the child learns to initiate interactions which are peaceable and pleasant rather than damaging. Some children will have already learnt these techniques before they attend pre-school, but not all of them, and it may be necessary for an adult to begin at the beginning in introducing the disruptive child to the pleasures of being with other people. This will involve working in very small groups, perhaps initially with the adult and one other child, until the disruptive child begins to develop the skills and confidence needed to get on with other children.

• Damage to Property

Some damage is accidental, the result of excitement or carelessness.

Some children seem to be unusually clumsy and leave a trail of damage in their wake. This is almost certainly not the child's fault and may be the result of a slight difficulty in motor co-ordination. Observations of the child's behaviour as a whole will indicate whether or not there is an overall problem that might require professional help.

Some kinds of damage might be a by-product of activities that are legitimate in themselves. A child who has been making "doughnuts" with the playdough may then choose to roll them in the sand tray in order to put "sugar" on them. This will do no good to the playdough and might result in the need to clean out the sand tray, but the child's intentions were not in themselves at fault – and indeed represent exactly the kind of exploratory behaviour we would want to encourage.

Deliberate and considered damage to property is more worrying. A child who breaks something in a sudden fit of anger may need help in finding other ways to express her feelings. If a child regularly attempts to damage the group's property, the adults need to give some thought to the reasons for this child's unhappiness and lack of commitment to the group. Regular observations, combined with an ongoing dialogue with parents, will often provide clues to the reasons behind the behaviour and to the approaches which will be of most help to the child.

• Physical or verbal abuse

The occasional quarrel is to be expected, though children should receive adult help in finding other ways to resolve their differences, but hitting or verbal abuse, especially sexist or racist abuse, is never acceptable. Immediate priority will be given to supporting and comforting the victim, but the child who makes a habit of such behaviour will be the subject of more long-term concerns. The adults will want to talk to the child's parents and to conduct their own observations to try to find out how to help.

Chapter 3. Defining problems

- ## Quietness

   This is a symptom that is sometimes overlooked, because it does not necessarily appear as a "problem" to busy adults. Nonetheless, a child who is too quiet and withdrawn may be even more urgently in need of help than one whose behaviour ensures a lot of adult attention. A child may be quiet simply through self-sufficient absorption in play, but in the case of an unusually quiet child, especially one who is very passive or takes little part in activities, the adults will want to observe to be sure that the quietness is not caused by fear or distress. The first line of enquiry, as always, will be to establish whether the child is equally quiet at home.

- ## Behaviour which puts the child at risk

   Some children expose themselves to danger just out of the need for physical challenge and excitement. Adults observing this must take steps to ensure that these needs are met in a safe way. There should always be in pre-school a succession of challenges available so children always have something new to go on to.

   Rarely, a child will seek danger for other reasons. A child who seems entirely indifferent to her own safety, or who indeed courts damage, may be suffering from a very serious lack of self esteem or may in other ways be deeply unhappy. Sometimes this behaviour may be linked with apparent rejection by the child of his or her gender, race or personal appearance. Children who persistently damage their own work, even when it is praised, are of concern for the same reason. Close observation is needed in co-operation with the child's parents, and it may be that professional help should be sought.

- ## Attention seeking

   Adult attention is necessary for children's physical and emotional well being; without it they could not survive. Some children seem to need more of it than others. Generally speaking, the child who constantly seeks attention is not getting enough of it. The adults will need to find ways of giving it in response to desirable behaviour rather than rewarding behaviour that is clearly designed just to seek attention.

The adults in the group may also want to ask themselves about the reasons for the child's need for an undue amount of attention. It may be that there is some source of unhappiness for which the child has no language but which drives him or her to seek comfort and support, albeit in inappropriate ways. Sometimes the problem is much simpler. A child from a very large family, in which adult attention has to be shared among a large number of children, may simply see the pre-school – quite rightly – as a place in which it is possible to catch up on adult company and conversation.

- **Aggressive play**

    Some aggression is necessary in life. Without it we would lack energy, initiative and determination. When we worry about "aggressive" play in children, what we are often talking about is the nature of their games. They may be trying to act out violent scenes, perhaps involving the use of weapons, which they have seen on television. Adults who feel very disturbed by this kind of play will need to find other themes which the children find equally exciting and stimulating. Perhaps a trip to the library to find out something about pirates or space rockets, together with some relevant additions to the dressing-up corner, might encourage the children to play a more acceptable game. However, games of this sort are often *about* aggression rather than being aggressive in themselves. In fact, the children may be engaged in a co-operative exercise, allocating roles to one another and agreeing together about the conduct of their imagined scene. This is different from play in which children show aggression towards one another.

Changes in behaviour

Behaviour which is normal for one child is not normal for another. An exuberant, excitable child who suddenly becomes passive and withdrawn needs watching just as much as a quiet, polite child who

Chapter 3. Defining problems

suddenly seems full of anger and aggression. In both cases, it is not the behaviour itself which is the problem, but the change in behaviour, which may be a symptom of a problem elsewhere.

Chapter 4
Assisting change

In an atmosphere of support and encouragement, children can be helped to change their behaviour, just as they can be helped to acquire new skills in other areas.

Scope for change

At any age, changing habits can be hard. Children will find it easier in an environment in which they feel personally valued and supported:

- It must always be clear, when a child is behaving in an unacceptable way, that it is the behaviour, not the child, which is unwelcome.
- Every opportunity must be taken to enhance children's self esteem and self confidence by recognising and praising their present achievements before helping them to move on to the next stage.
- It is important to leave open the door to change. Labelling children can limit the possibilities by creating a set of assumptions about them which may be self-fulfilling.

For example, if the adults start to say of a particular child or a particular group of children – "All they want to do is run around on the toy cars," there is a danger that those children will be eventually steered towards that one kind of activity. Adults may gradually stop inviting them to join in with music, constructional play or board games, and the children's choice – and their opportunities for change – will be limited.

When a particular child seems to need help with several aspects of behaviour at once, there is a risk that if the adults try to tackle all the difficult areas at the same time, the child will be constantly "under

Chapter 4. Assisting change

attack" and will find it hard to make adjustments in so many areas at a time.

In this case, the adults need to get together to establish priorities. If a child refuses to sit still, hits other children and uses unacceptable language, the first priority will be to protect other children, so a concerted effort will be made to help the child make better relationships with one or more other children, to ensure that there is no opportunity to hurt them and to find other ways for the child to express angry feelings – through conversation, through creative or imaginative play, or through physical activity.

Records will be kept to detect any pattern which will give a clue to the reasons for such behaviour. Once an agreed course of intervention has been set in motion by the adults, the records will also help to show whether the chosen approach is being successful. This can be very important. Adults also need confidence and reassurance in tackling a difficult task. If they are tempted to despair after a bad morning it can help morale to look back over the records and see that, over the week or month, instances of this kind of undesirable behaviour are decreasing.

Adults who have worked in this way to "target" one aspect of a child's behaviour often report that the other difficult behaviours start to diminish at the same time without any particular focus on them being needed. This suggests that a range of unacceptable behaviours may all stem from the same cause. To help the child tackle one problem successfully brings the others under control too.

Intervening

In addition to long term planning, pre-school workers need techniques for dealing on the spot with situations as they arise.

The high ratio of adults to children in pre-school is invaluable in ensuring that undesirable situations are detected quickly, before they have time to develop too far.

Behaviour in pre-school groups

Children need to know that if things go wrong, an adult will always intervene. This knowledge forms part of their security in the group. When a child starts behaving in a way which is unacceptable, there are several things to tackle:

- Other children may be hurt and upset, or distracted from what they are doing.
- The noise level may rise.
- The group's equipment may be at risk.
- The group's rules must be seen to be upheld. Otherwise all the children will become uncertain about them.

The adults will need to operate as a team to ensure that all aspects of the situation are covered. The inappropriate behaviour must be stopped and one adult will have to take care of the child in question. It may be that a reminder is all that is necessary.

Children sometimes misbehave without really meaning to. Adults can create a positive and helpful atmosphere by recognising this and approaching with a positive, 'Try doing it this way' rather than a negative, 'Don't do that'.

If a particular piece of equipment is being abused in some way, the group may have a system of withdrawing the child from that activity for a while. Children themselves, if the rules of the group are discussed with them, see this as "fair." It is important, however, to help the child find something else to do and to give her/him adult support, if necessary, in settling down to it.

If any damage has been done – if, for example, sand or water have been spilled or blocks scattered – the child can be helped to put things right. This is not a "punishment" but simply an illustration of cause and effect within the group: if a mess is created, it has to be cleared.

If the child is very angry and upset, it may be that "time out" is necessary. This means a short spell away from the other children and activities in the company of one adult who can provide space and calm – and, if necessary, a cuddle – to enable the child to come to terms with the situation. The child needs to know:

Chapter 4. Assisting change

- that such behaviour will always be stopped
- the reasons why it is not acceptable to behave that way
- that the child herself is still wanted and valued
- that adult help will be available to help the child avoid such behaviour in future
- that if the unacceptable behaviour arose from strong feelings of anger or frustration, there is nothing wrong with the feelings themselves, only the way in which they were expressed.

Sometimes, observing a child's difficulty in coming to terms with strong feelings such as anger, the adults will try to ensure in the group as a whole that there are opportunities to handle large and heavy objects, to engage in messy activities, to bang clay and squeeze dough, to respond to loud or fast music and to paint with a range of strong colours. On other occasions it may be appropriate for the adults taking time out with the child to recommend directly to the child that when he/she feels this way in the future, one of these activities would be a more appropriate way of expressing those feelings.

Meanwhile, other members of staff will be looking after the other children. The first priority, if any child has been hurt or frightened or is the victim of racist or sexist abuse, is the support and comfort of that child. The next priority is to calm and reassure all the other children as necessary and to get the whole group back to their normal play and learning. This is important for them, and it also ensures that the child who caused the disturbance has a calm and ordered environment to return to if he/she has had time out.

It is better to prevent unacceptable behaviour than to have to correct it. Alert adults can often step in with a distraction to prevent a play situation from deteriorating or to prevent a problem by anticipating it.

Regular observations and record-keeping will sometimes reveal that one child cannot deal acceptably with a particular situation or activity. Some children, for example, find large group activities such as 'circle time' very hard to cope with. In this case, it is better not to allow an undesirable pattern to develop of repeated, inappropriate behaviour which the adults then have to deal with to the detriment of the group situation as a whole. An adult will need to keep the child company in a parallel occupation for a while – perhaps, if the group is having a music session, doing a few finger rhymes on a one-to-one basis – until he or she is ready to join the main group, perhaps at first for just a short while.

Some children find an enforced change of activity so disruptive of their security and concentration that they cannot then settle properly to anything else. A warning that a game will have to come to an end soon can help these children adjust.

Punishments which hurt or humiliate a child, such as smacking, shaking or the use of a "naughty chair" will not be used in pre-schools. In a group situation, such abuse of adult power can do nothing to build up an environment of mutual trust, respect and kindness.

Working with parents

In behaviour as in all other matters, the child's own parents are the key source of information and insight about the child.

If some aspect of a child's behaviour worries the group, the parents will be the first ones to know. There is no question of "complaining" about a child's behaviour; the pre-school leader or keyworker will consult the parents as the experts in their own child's background and behaviour, so that their insights may be added to those of the group in building up a joint strategy to help the child. In a group where staff and parents keep joint records, this sharing of expertise becomes routine.

When a group approaches a parent for further information or advice about a child's behaviour, the parent may be astonished to find that the child is acting very differently in pre-school from the way she/he behaves at home. If this is the case, staff and parents together can consider what it is about the pre-school situation which is making a difference. (Sometimes the position is reversed: in a group which genuinely respects the input of parents, a mother or father will feel able to say, "I wish......would eat/draw/play like that at home." Then the staff and parents can look together about aspects of the pre-school approach which might also work at home.)

Sometimes an inquiry from the group may confirm parents' own anxieties. Some parents in this position will want to deny that there is anything amiss; others will welcome the chance to discuss something which may have been troubling them for some time. It must always be clear that the group is not making judgements, about the children or about their families; what the group is aiming to do is to concentrate all available adult resources in order to help the child.

Working closely with parents has advantages also when rewarding and reinforcing desirable behaviour on the part of the child. Passing on to a parent at the end of the day or session the good news that their child has concentrated for longer than ever before, or passed the pieces of apple around at snack time, or been especially helpful to another child, means that the child gets praise twice for the same accomplishment. In addition, it sends parent and child home feeling pleased, and opens up the possibility that the same good behaviour may now be expected and rewarded at home.

Occasionally, changes in a child's behaviour may be explained by the parents in terms of sources of stress at home. These may include illness, financial problems or difficulties within a marriage. It would be important in these circumstances to establish clearly whom the information may be shared with. If parents wish it to go no further, they must be confident that their wishes will be respected.

Seeking additional help

Sometimes the combined efforts of staff and parents may not be sufficient to enable a child to make the necessary changes. In this case, outside help may be necessary and it is useful for the group to have built up contacts with health visitors, social services representatives, educational psychologists and other professionals in the area. With the parents' consent, a health visitor or other professional may be able to make an initial observation of the child in the pre-school situation. This can give a clearer picture of the child, and of any difficulties, than trying to obtain information about the child in the impersonal setting of an office or clinic.

Seeking outside help must never be regarded as a failure on the part of group or parent. On the contrary, it indicates a responsible approach by the adults, ensuring that support available within the community is channelled to help a child who needs it.

Working with children

The group is there to help each child to develop as fully as possible in all areas. This includes opportunities to build up social skills and to learn behaviour that will enable the child to go into the wider world with confidence.

In a good pre-school, children are learning above all what they *can* do. In an environment where their legitimate needs for security, challenge and stimulus are met, where there is plenty of adult company and support, and where a few understandable rules are kindly and consistently applied, children learn that acceptable behaviour is something they can do.

It will not always be easy and it will always be more difficult for some children than for others. In pre-school, children will be helped to find acceptable ways to express strong feelings and will have the reassurance of discovering, through stories and conversations, that other people can feel that way too.

Above all, children will be enabled to feel that this is their group, a place in which they are individually valued and to which they each have their own special contribution to make. Within this secure and nurturing framework, both children and adults are free to grow and change.

Signs on boxes,

signs on jars,

signs on gates,

signs on cars,

signs on billboards,

signs on trees,

signs on t-shirts,
signs on me.